Love, Pain, and Other Things

Featuring the poem, "I Cry."

Joe Evener

ISBN - 9798846165540

Cover design by: Joe Evener through Canva
Library of Congress Control Number: 2018675309
Printed in the United States of America

Dedication

To my wife.

Bronwen, without your constant love and support, I could have never started this dream let alone complete it. With all my love, thank you!

Acknowledgement

To my readers.

Thank you for allowing my written words to come into your life. I hope you find inspiration for whatever journey you are on.

There are no rules to writing poetry,
just a passion for the art!

Love, Pain, and Other Things

Joe Evener

I Cry

I cry for the lonely and the weak
I cry for the people without a means to speak
I cry for the girl who lost all of her friends
I cry for the children whose pain never ends
I cry for the inflicted, the addicted, and the dying
I cry for the children living in fear
Who lost a parent while protecting those things we all hold dear.
I cry for the young who are sick, and for the unborn
I cry for a world that has been torn
apart by war, racism, oppression, bigotry, and violence
I cry for those who work in silence
with little to show and hungry mouths to feed
The unloved, the abandoned, and those in need
I cry for those who believe in the lies
of false promises and the lure of an easy prize.
I cry for those who need comfort when they are kicked down
I cry for mankind. I cry for freedom. I cry for healing those who are lost and need to be found.

The Sea

Send me to the sea or any Great Lake
Take me to the landless home of my father
wherever the mighty waves break.

I want to feel the salty sting of ocean air
and the spray of mist over mast.
See the frolic of mermaids with golden hair
as the roar of bell bottom trousers the
code of navy-blue echoes over the quiet vast.

The sea, a port for the polarity of my soul:
calming yet wild, beautiful, and dangerous,
I climb the rigging as the storm clouds roll.

Gone from the harbor, out to sea
memories of ancient mariners
buried under me.
Whether from weather, plunder, or wars of old
'Neath the watery gray-blue coffin
their stories left untold.

Send me to the sea or any Great Lake
Take me to the landless home of my father
wherever the mighty waves break.

Winter Morn

Fog lifts over a wintry morn.
There is a beauty to our love
as new as the day we uttered those words.

It burns fierce and bright in the light
of when dreams become reality,
reality becomes romance, and
romance becomes reminiscing.

Listen to the words of the poet.
The pain rests deep within,
but the trueness remains:
hearts crave hearts,
souls crave souls,
flesh craves flesh.

I sleep stirred in the knowledge that
dawn will come.

Lily

From my window I have a spectacular view. The dawn of a new spring embraces her heavenly daughter, a lovely lily in bloom. I look after my little lily, fragile in so many ways. Yet, weathering storm after storm, grows stronger with each passing day.

A better man a sonnet of love would render, of the strong and mysterious force in the magic of such breathtaking splendor. My little one blooms smooth and innocent. I wish I were a mere butterfly that I could enjoy her texture so delicate.

How can a single object display feelings mischievous and raw? Never understanding how or why, the beauty of it all. With intoxicating fragrance that brings pleasure and desire, the essence of nature's perfect gift. The fair lily gives my heart delight and becomes my daimon. My life breath.

In darkness the dear lily bathes in the moonlight. A moonbeam displays my fond little flower's elegance to an audience of one in the twilight. At daybreak like a sleeping princess, it rises and awakes. The dew of morning lingers and caresses her soft, tender petals like the sweat from a lover's skin. My petite flower appears flush with excitement as wind plays a sweet melody and dances between its limbs.

No other blossom is so flawless and exquisite. Standing firm, the precious flower glows majestic in the handiwork of God it is easy to believe, when watching the purity of my lily so sweet.

Book of Dreams

An open book - I read about her life. I feel the pain through the beauty of her light.

I turn the page. Her love revealed before my very eyes.
I am amazed. She holds my hand as I tremble at her side.
I turn the page. Her laughter seduces me I know.

The romance grows. I stare, lost in her eyes of green and gold. I read of dreams. Magic desires along a garden wall of love. I hear the sound; sweet music of two souls as they touch.

Her fire burns. This passion cannot hide. When I'm with her fantasies fill my night. Our bodies rise. Her hair flows down like rain. I kiss her lips, the burning of eternal flames.
Enchanted times, her spirit carries me away. Her loving gaze, in the spring I feel the winds of change.

I turn the page; the suspense of jealous skies. Like a bird, she can't help but fly. The glow of her smile warms my darkest days.Reading every precious word, as I continue to turn every page.

I read of wonder; hoping to break the strings of fate. I turn the page; hoping for one last dance.
We say goodbye as the story starts to end. I turn to cry; as time runs from my hands.

The Long Run

I run to feel free - no demons, no
dragons chasing me.

I could solve the world's problems, or just solve
mine, perhaps forget them all and
leave the world behind.

In the cold of winter or with the summer
heat beating down - muscles ache,
heart pumping faster, sweat
dripping on the ground.

I soar like an eagle and sprint like a falling star;
to be calm, happy, content with life
and the way things are.

Being one with God - my conflicted soul,
in the moments of truth, peace of mind is my goal.

Experience life as it comes, one mile at a time
inspired as I am with my thoughts alone
traveling this long road home.

Passion

Listen, it speaks to me. It guides my every move, my every action. I listen. I have no choice. It calls me again and again.

The anticipation grows in me. Moving me closer to you than I could ever imagine. It makes my insides quake in nervous pleasure.

This feeling laid dormant deep in my soul waiting to escape from its prison. It is the origin of everything done in the world: love, hate, pleasure, and pain. It is why writers write, lovers love, and singers sing. It wounds and it heals. Wars are fought because of it. With it we may never find peace, without it we would surely die.

How this thing was born, no man will know the secret. It rules everything and anything it touches. It grows slowly and spreads through my body, like the wings of an eagle. Once set free it will never return. Circling, soaring above the clouds. It searches for you.

I watch adoringly as you close your eyes. The sparkle and warmth trapped in them light up the celestial night. The soft, gentle touch of your lips makes my heart pound so loud I wonder how you cannot hear it. I want to hold you forever, protecting you, comforting you, making you a part of me.

There you stand. You cloak yourself in the shadows of darkness, yet your face shines bright with an air of play. Caught in my gaze. Your undeniable beauty manifests itself to me. Feelings I can barely contain. We are forever forged as one. Transcending all bliss.

You are pure as a snowflake, soft as a petal in bloom. My life illuminates in your radiant presence. A warm inviting smile like the dawn of a brand-new day.
The tips of my fingers stroke slow and lovingly across the soft landscape of your back. It is impossible to catch my breath as I hear the sound of an uncontainable moan escape your lips. How can it be that you can crush my world with a single sigh?

You are my lover with the tender touch of silk. Serious when needed, caring, loving, kind, and gentle. Deep and thoughtful in ways beyond your years. Insightful to all that is around.

We have become one in mind, body, and spirit. A moment eternally emblazed in my mind's eye. The craving of your body lingers over me. This thing that calls me, this passion. It sweeps over us like the wind.

We will persevere. That is my promise. And I will spend the rest of my life unlocking the mystery of you.

You

I see the snow falling, pure white and full of wonder.

I see the rain coming; see the lightning hear the thunder.

I see the world around me and the awe it should bring.

When I close my eyes, I still see you, but I can't feel a thing.

I hear the crickets chirping, the sound fills the night.

I hear the children laughing, with smiles big and bright.

A chorus of voices and the words they want to sing.

I hear the sound of your laughter, but I can't feel a thing.

There's so much I want to tell you, and not is taking its toll

I gave you all I have, my spirit, my heart and my soul.

My mouth still longs to kiss you, the joy it would bring.

Yes.

My heart's still pounding, but I can't feel a thing.

My Lady of Light

Two worlds collide. Lost in the gaze of lover's eyes.

No boundaries for a beauty so fair,
My Lady of Light. Ballad plays in the
constellation of night.

I shake at her touch, so soft and gentle, a feather
caress. Moved by her soul, her spirit, her mind,
and her kiss.

Two bodies moving in rhythm. A sonnet of rhyme.
A symphony of passion, as temperature does climb.

The taste of her body and mouth, while her tongue
beckons to play and thrill as never before.
Her body of smooth pearl, glistens like dew
on a new morn.

I seize every second the same as an hour,
like a warm summer rain falls on a spring flower.

The force of a deluge pours over my body with
The essence of her. She trembles and moans,
bodies soaked, hearts speed akin to hummingbird.

Too many sunsets have I missed in her garden with
roses in bloom. Lost in her afterglow, her
Eyes sparkle in the radiance of the night.
She is my springtime, my soul mate,
My lover, My Lady of Light.

Shadow of a Rose

The shadow of a rose dances in the morning light.

I wake with these cravings from dreams of last night.

Time flies too fast for reality seems.

Flush with passion and desire it brings.

Her taste lingers in my mouth,

her scent on my body.

We share the sun, the heavenly warm sun.

I am under the spell of her breathtaking beauty.

I wake with a fever burning out of control.

Sweat dripping, the soft pleasure of her moan.

Longing for more of you and the wonderful things you do to me.

Her fingers find my back, releasing my energy.

Another night is gone. Lost in delight.

I wake from these cravings from last night's dreams.

As the shadow of a rose dances in the morning light.

One

Fire burns under porcelain skin,

bodies tremble and souls quake to contain the sensations within.

Two hearts, two souls we become the flesh of intertwining spirits

unite as one.

I taste her mouth of ambrosia and feel her running through my veins.

Sweet, honeyed nectar my life force no longer the same.

Thoughts of her come upon me like waves crashing in the sea.

All that she is, is all that I need.

Quiet meadows plush with green, valleys of flowers and a gentle stream.

Where doeth my love take me, I have not a care.

The silent sky, the jealous stars, lost in her stare.

The passionate sound of two hearts

sharing a beat. One breath, one

heart, one soul we meet.

Closer to Me

Creamy white, smooth like glass,

eternal Eros of my essence.

Lost in reflection, not moments past,

I see nothing but her presence.

I can't look from her eyes.

Delicate and slow, I feel her body rise.

Wings upon the wind I ride.

Caught in her glow,

stirring in her light.

Unlocking the mysteries

Of my soul that cannot be seen.

On and on you whisper in my dreams.

Close enough to hear her softly cry,

The tempest of her lullaby.

Gentle spirit dancing like

A prisoner set free.

Captured in silence 'til

You come closer to me.

Gentle Rain

Gentle rain fall on me, ease my
mind from its memories.

Gentle rain cleanse my soul and
wash away all I know.

Your abstract shapes shine like
mica upon the ground.

Soaking wet, it hides the tears

I never show as the stream drizzles down.

Gentle rain, will I survive the downpour of
the storm you bring? At times like a

maelstrom and others soft, soothing,
and warm showers of spring.

Like tender kisses on my skin - the rainfall

Refreshes and renew my thoughts
like the flowers in bloom.

Oh, how I love a gentle rain.

JOE EVENER

Morning Comes

Morning comes, another day
Following another night without you.
Have you had those moments when you don't
know what to do?
I stand on the edge of time
Tears in my eyes remembering when
you were mine.
I face the day a shadow of man
in the pouring rain.
Strangers pass by and they
can't see the pain.
I never realized how much I wanted to stop you
But I couldn't stop you.
Do you still feel me by your side?
Why did you run away and hide?
I will remember you all my life
You appear in my dreams
I see you dance in a new moon
through my window
Then you're gone, I'm left as cold as ice.

My Soul Sang

(from my novel, "Seducing Bronwyn")

Bronwyn, I dreamt of her in my mind as the sun softly set.
I felt her presence in my heart with the rhythm of my breath.
I heard her whispers ride the wind
eye to eye
lips to lips
I lost myself in her body
My soul sang for her with a song of life with no end.

Castle by the Sand

I sit upon a rocky shore in my castle by the sand.
Haunted by your sacred kiss no one else would understand.
We laughed and whispered sweet lullabies with amatory
sighs and your smiling eyes in my castle by the sand.
Stars burn interluding dreams of you in my castle by the sand
Dreams not wanting another tomorrow of our future plans
I breathe in your kisses that have me undone and rushing
over me with your ardor tongue in my castle by the sand
Blushing words stole my heart that quickened at your sight
When will those words, those dreams, those nights of visions
kissing you and entangled limbs entwine I don't want to be
without your body nearer to mine in my castle by the sand.
For many a time and more to come of stolen glances in a
crowded room staring, longing in your pools of Venusian
eyes I must wait for our time to bloom with lucid dreams
of us dancing alone your hand in mine not meant to be
until you break the cursed ties that bind will you escape
with me and join me in my castle in the sand?
Alas, it is not to be. I must wait for you, I muse
Holding back my fantasy flies. I can't deny you.
until you are mine and mine alone in my castle by the sand.
For you were the forbidden wave that rushed and crushed my
soul, my heart
So I tarry on rebuilding my castle in the sand.

Whisper to my Soul

Whisper to my soul, oh nature's muse.
I watch white pappus or winged fairies dance,
and rustled leaves shiver with God's own breath.
Morning dew awakes on vibrant green blades
as I sit beneath canopied trees.
Glimmering shafts of light sparkle on crescent
waves, glowing on a golden pond.

Discarded

Discarded, waiting, longing as time fades. Don't let light darken your dreams. Find purpose in what you are doing until you find why you were placed here or there. We are all where we need to be until time commands us to be somewhere else. Thrive in each moment. Thrive and rejoice in circumstances, even those beyond your control. Each fragment of sand in an hourglass is gold worth. What will you do with your precious grains? Be a prince among men, or a queen among commoners. Don't fade away slowly waiting for the end, the long night, the closing of the sepulcher.

Old Country Roads

The feel of a country road, dust kicking up for miles,

cornfields as far as the eye can see;

a nice little hiding place for you and me.

Warm summer breeze blowing through

this mind of mine,

thoughts of sweat, limbs, and blanket intwined.

Long tan legs, silky hair and matching mischievous

eyes;

velvet lips plump that glisten and sigh.

I miss those days being young, wild, and free.

You and me and cornfields as far as the eye can see.

Into the Wild

Into the wild, into the unknown, that is where the brave
play.

Do not stay locked in your fears, hiding from the storms,
safe on the shore. Do not be afraid to roam, to fly, to love.
Make a way that is true to your heart, consoling
to your soul, and pleasing to your mind. Run on
winged feet into the wild, free your spirit into
the unknown. Chase your heart with unrelenting
passion and be the one others want to follow.

"The Easiest Lie"
(From "The Heart of Seras" series, book 4, "The Dark Warrior")

The easiest lie might be

to say it's not important (when it is to me)

Or, I don't need him (but I do)

I don't love him (though it's true)

It wasn't my fault, whatever it was

I can't let go of the past because...

I would be happy if I only had

My life is the worst and it makes me sad

I could stop or start at any time

Everyone's life is better than mine

If only I had more (this list could be endless)

'It doesn't matter' is a worn out mess

Saying 'I don't have a choice' isn't very wise

What we tell ourselves are the easiest lies.

Oh, My Playful Muse

Oh, my playful muse, what stories have I dreamt?
Cherubs blush at the nocturnal eves I have spent.
I sing praises of your beauty as my silent soul cries.
The hunter's moon reflects from your viridian eyes.
Like two oceans sparkling with deviltry delight.
Surrender my doubt with trembled voice in the night.
A bee's temporal visit to flower sweet bliss.
Come melt me with the sweet honey from your lips.
A carnal serenade tangled in silk and skin
Sighs whispered from candied lips begin
Vigorous passion radiates essence craved
Limbs linger, sparks ignite, lovers saved
Wisps falling on petite, creamy skin glistened from above
Two are entwined with poetic pulsating rhythm of love.
Amidst darkened skies
dancing candlelight reflect
as heaving breasts rise
Inch by inch, my flesh traces yours
Taking me in, enveloping my love.
Look at the stars. Are they the cause of my strangled cry?
No, it is you, my jewel, my flower, my dove.

My Soul

My soul, my soul lays exposed. Night descends dressed in raven black cloak.

Midnight whispers your name in the sweet, shadowed hour; soft, gentle, warm with immense power.

Moonlight reflects through orbs of golden sheen, prowling like a creature for her prey with hungry gleam.

Two silhouettes across a dark horizon meet, catching elusive breath of fear, excitement, and uncontrolled belief.

The polite invitation of your parted lips beckons me so close I can't resist.

Anticipation runs down my spine as we share our first kiss.

My soul, my soul lays exposed. Night descends dressed in raven black cloak.

Midnight on the Edge of Hell

Know my heart O'lovely Muse, daughter of
memories.
This darkest of all nights when heroes fall.
Soothe my soul and calm my madness, her
words spoke to me with the singing of a goddess.

A night heavy with liquid air, thick as blood.
Give me safe harbor from rumor and deceit.
My thoughts move rapidly as water through a
river. Keep my course while the clouds shift and the
tempest blows like God's own breath.

Keeping alive my flames of passion and pain.
I burn to know of my ancient homeland
and the bitter war brought forth. Trumpets
echo resounding nerve, with war horses raining
down on fallen walls. I pray for their prey.

I must stand to be counted my sweet Erato.
I take up my arms and ease my lover's soul
with an oath true as if made on the banks of Styx.
Aurora rises from her time spent beneath
Night wearing robes embroidered in gold.

On the blood of my father I give my pledge to
dearest swift Mercury - my patron god - deliver
in haste the news of my fate. My words vanish
in the air as the jealous sun smiles on me.

Morning Rises

I am awake. My long sleep is done.
The dream was sweet, but sometimes long.
I fought to escape when the dream turned wrong.
She lies there. Perfect.
How beautiful. How pure.
I want to wake her but will wait a while more.
Her hair of silky brown falls softly like a river flowing
Down.
Her face, oh her face. Either a wake or not full of happiness and love.
I can't wait much longer - and as I do I thank my God above.
I can taste her breath, a taste so sweet
I envy the lips they pass, lips I want again to meet.
Just a kiss. Just a taste.
Her lips her lips; soft, wet and
Full of wonderness.
Morning is not so beautiful as she.
The flames blaze bright in her now sleeping
Eyes. Only when closed can the stars
Fill the darkened skies.
Is it still a dream? Am I still asleep?
Does she really exist?
My morning rises and greets me with
A kiss.

King of Dreamers

Standing in the calm of a sky brilliant with stars
truth comes in the night as I hold you in my arms
the sweet smell of honey suckle does surround
with not another single flower around.

A golden streak rips the quiet sky
an orange burst rising from the night
I catch a tear from your eyes I dry.

I close my eyes in the night to see your face
remembering the lips with my finger I did once
trace.

A kiss soft and slow as the rain falls gently down
to hold your face in my hands, staring feverishly
without
making a sound.

In the power, magic, and beauty of love I do believe
I watched many nights as the king of dreamers
spell he did weave.

You are beautiful, gorgeous, and precious just as I
remember
as I carry you up to our room.
The sacrifices made, I told you I would
find a way. And I will know when I
get there, the only dream that mattered finally
came true - I am with you.

3 Unspoken Words

The moon rises bright and full, right for the hunter.

Words are a window to my soul, within
them there's no wonder.

Feelings like a morning fog, covering my
memory. Caught amid burning ambers I
can't stand the cold of misery.

Silent screams pass by unknowing ears, I cry, though
no one listens - pierce the longing of the passing years.

Laying awake in the quiet dark, thoughts
of you crawl upon me like a spider.

I can't let go, I cannot hide. No, I cannot fight her.

I won't say what you do not want to hear, I won't
tell you what I long to say, you know my every look
and thought, will there come another day?

Do you think of me on sleepless nights, or
when the sun fills a begging sky?

Do you think of me when the warm wind blows,
or when the rustic leaves fall to die?

For you I would swim the river Styx, or give up
all but one dream. I miss you my playful friend,
Good Puck has nothing on me. For you I would
do this and more, You know it's very true.

Even when I never say it......

Inspired by Psalms 23

I want to dwell with you Lord through each passing day,
you are my lifeblood; all on the alter I gladly lay.

Your mercy and grace surround me, as I walk into the dark cold void of the night,
my enemies do tremble and flee at your sight

They cannot harm me with their tools of lies and deceit,
I can be evil, or I can be good - in my shame I fall at your feet.

Why do I fall, why do I fail, why do I forget about the scars from the nails?

Restore my soul, oh Lord I pray,
You are always there to keep me on the path of your way.

Nothing but you sweet calming love can quench the desires of my life before.

In your Holy Love I shall want no more.

The Warrior's Journey

The battle defines me, I am a warrior.
I march onto the frozen path, a small dusting of snow covering the grass. Patient warrior, not knowing how long the time will last.
Two years, three years, four? I wonder to myself. Tired warrior, rise to battle once more.
My secret fear, my hidden pain, it is up to God or fate if I should ever return and see her again. And, if so, how will time have changed us? Doubting warrior, faith in God is a must.
I hate the winter. How many have there been? Sometime it feels too long and then again at times it feels like yesterday. How many friends have I lost? How many times have I cheated fate? The battle against the unknown is a tragic cost.
On these long cold days, I think about the enemy. Am I winning? Am I losing? Is the fighting going as planned? When will the battle end? Angry warrior, make another stand.
In the stories of old it is pride that ends all good men. Proud warrior, pray that it is not your end.
Is love and war the only two things men really know? All I have with me is my sword and my word. Passionate warrior, her love makes a third.
A trophy to behold, such as Grendel's shoulder I bare. When this moment ends, I will return to my beloved so fair. Foolish warrior, battle defines me.

I am a warrior.

The Value of Everything

I don't understand weeding. Who is to say which plants are pretty and useful, and which are weeds?
Is it the practicality?
The prettiness?
What makes one different than the other?
The same could be said of gems. What makes one rock more special than another?
Someone decided that gold is pretty and valuable.
Someone decided diamonds are pretty
thereby making them valuable.
Emeralds, rubies, sapphires, the whole lot of them are valuable because someone said so
because of their attractiveness.
That brings me to beauty.
Someone decided what is attractive and what is not,
therefore what is decided becomes true.
A weed, a stone, a lovely person can all be considered priceless if your mindset is shifted,
and you look for the beauty and value of all things within themselves.

About The Author

Joe Evener

Joe Evener is a graduate of The Ohio State University and received his master's degree from Mt. Vernon Nazarene University 2011. A long-time high school track and field coach, and wrestling coach Joe became a teacher in 2014.

His love of reading was inspired by his mother. He wrote his first story in fourth grade and never looked back. Joe has written several newspaper articles and has been featured in poetry compilations. In 2005, he began working on THE HEART OF SERAS series.

Joe loves to travel with his wife, Bronwen. They have been married 40 years, and live in Marengo, Ohio. They have two sons, Joey and Jacob. Jacob has two sons, Jake and Jamison.

Books By This Author

The Heart Of Seras: Journey To Seras

Julie Ayers is a normal fifteen year old living in the quiet town of Sunset, Ohio. Her world is turned upside down by the arrival of the school's new teacher, Marcus Campbell.

Marcus Campbell has a secret. He is a warrior from a medieval dimension searching for the mythical "Heart"-a hero given to the people of Seras to rid their world of impending evil. Marcus's quest is challenged when he realizes that the "Heart" is the vibrant teenage girl. Now, against his better judgment, he must try convincing Julie to go to his world and begin preparation to face whatever evil lies ahead.

Journey to Seras is the first book in the six part The Heart of Seras fantasy series. It begins the adventures of the two unlikely heroes as they battle the dark forces of Seras.

Also avaiable on Audible

The Heart Of Seras: The Elders

Julie Ayer's freshman year of high school ended horribly. Now Marcus Campbell must try to convince her to return to Seras to learn the secrets of Seras from the mysterious immortal, Redderick Bobo. Going back to Seras is the last thing on Julie's mind. She wants no part of Seras, or her teacher. What secrets does Redderick Bobo have to tell? Who were the Elders known as "The Five Lions of God"? Why is Julie Ayers the chosen savior of Seras?

Only returning to the dreaded dimension will answer these questions and more for Julie. Can she bring herself to forgive Marcus, and return to Seras? The future of Seras and Earth depends on it.

Also available on Audible

The Heart Of Seras: Revelation

The first half of Julie Ayers' junior year is going horribly wrong. Balancing life between Earth and Seras is taking its toll on her. She doesn't know who she can trust, her best friends are fighting, her basketball coach is harassing her, and things are about to get a lot worse.

As Julie already struggles to figure out the meaning behind Redderick Bobo calling her the "Betrothed", a much deadly secret is suddenly revealed that will shake her to the core.

The Heart Of Seras: The Dark Warrior

Julie now knows Marcus's secret. Her personal life is a disaster and Marcus is missing. He needs to confront his past with the fear it might change him for the worst. Can Julie forgive Marcus in time to save him from himself?

Love, Pain, and Other Things

Love, Pain, and Other Things is a compilation of poetry written over the last twenty years. It covers topics of love, heartbreak, remembering days of long ago, and everything in between.

There are so many inspirations for this book, it would be difficult to state just one. I hope you enjoy reading the different prose as much as I enjoyed writing them and reliving them as I created this book.

Joe

www.ingramcontent.com/pod-product-compliance
Lightning Source LLC
La Vergne TN
LVHW052107160826
845678LV00015B/3413

* 9 7 9 8 8 4 6 1 6 5 5 4 0 *